MEDITATIONS
IN THE
UPPER ROOM

By The Most Rev. Dr. Charles Jason Gordon
Archbishop of Port of Spain

Sophronismos Press
Louisville, Kentucky

First Printing: November 2019
ISBN: 978-1-7335457-2-3

ADDRESS:
27 Maraval Rd
Maraval
Trinidad and Tobago
Caribbean

Email: abcjg@catholictt.org

Cover photos used with permission.
Dahlgren Chapel of the Sacred Heart
Office of Campus Ministry
Georgetown University

CONTENTS

MEDITATIONS
IN THE
UPPER ROOM

ACKNOWLEDGEMENTS

I would like to thank the Jesuit community of Georgetown University for hosting me during my retreat in July 2019. You provided an amazing space for prayer, reflection and contemplation during my days with you. Thanks also to Rev. Dr. Gerard McGlone SJ who directed my retreat. By inviting me to the Upper Room with Mary, you pointed the way to a portal leading to mystery, love and indescribable grace. Your direction and encouragement led me to ponder these mysteries and to the text that follows.

Thanks also to the Office of Campus Ministry, Georgetown University who gave me permission to use the photo of the stained glass windows on the front cover and in the book. A picture is worth 1000 words. Thank you!

I would like to also thank my proofreaders, Ms. Kathleen Maharaj and Simone Delochan who laboured through the text several times to bring it to completion.

A deep debt of gratitude to Fr. Ronald Knott who has assisted me in the publishing process and Tim Schoenbachler, who designed the book, and made it ready for printing.

To Mary, mother of the church, and mother of all disciples who want to be beloved of Jesus. Your maternal care for your son as he hung upon the cross continues to be a source of inspiration and grace for me as we witness the Church being crucified in our days. Intercede for us, that like you we will have the grace to live these days with courage and hope. But most of all, lead us, the modern disciples, to Jesus and His Father, who continues to surprise us with incredible love, patience and care.

PREFACE

"Love is shown more in deeds than in words."
Saint Ignatius of Loyola

It is an honor to write this preface for "Meditations in the Upper Room," written by His Grace, Archbishop Jason Gordon of Port of Spain, Trinidad and Tobago. You too will be moved and consoled as I have been by what is written here. It is rare gift to have someone take us into a new journey of faith, hope and healing. These days it is exactly what we need especially in light of the many crises in our Church and in our society. These contemplations that you are about to read are filled with a stunning and sacred intimacy that you are about tó be privileged to see, hear and know. You will be able to see, touch and feel the early Church as never before. You will see, touch and feel love.

For Saint Ignatius of Loyola, all forms of prayer were about finding and experiencing God' love. As such, "contemplation" was a key form of prayer. "Ignatian Contemplation" is a form of prayer in which you place yourself in a gospel scene. It uses all the tools of your imagination. As one example, imagine that you are at the Sea of Galilee when Jesus calls His disciples, what do you feel, see and hear? Where are you in this scene? One might be helped by asking quite simple and direct questions: what do you see, what do you hear, what do you feel, where are you, as you contemplate this scene? What desires rise in you as you pray?

It is interesting that in the fourth week of the *Spiritual Exercises*, St Ignatius of Loyola askes the retreatant (excersitant) to "contemplate" or enter the scene when Mary, the Mother of God meets the Risen Lord for the first time after the Resurrection. We have no written version of this encounter in the Synoptic tradition but for Ignatius and the retreatant you are asked to imagine what surely must have happened. Imagine for a second, the Blessed Mother after the crucifixion, *La Dolorosa*, in tears, in shock, perhaps numb and still in her blooded mantle (robes) that once held the body of her beloved Son. Now, imagine her Son who has risen appearing to her. What do you hear them say, what do they do, what do you hear, what do you see? The following pages will give you a glimpse into what must have happened at that moment in their relationship. These pages will also challenge you to go to places that you may have never I imagined as possible. You will enter the Upper Room perhaps as never before.

The Upper Room is central to a Christian's identity and to the identity of the Church. Mary, Jesus's mother is also central to each of us and to the very beginning of the Christian community. So much happened in this place: Eucharist, the foundation of priestly identity, the washing of the feet and yet also a place of betrayal, confusion, and being locked in fear. The first letter of John expresses this quite directly:

"What was from the beginning, what we have heard, what we have seen with our eyes, what we looked upon and touched with our hands concerns the Word of life."

1 John 1:1. (New American Bible Translation)

I pray that as you read and pray over these scenes and these words that you might experience the very grace that descended upon the disciples gathered with Mary in the Upper Room. May you hear and feel that unique "Upper Room" grace when Jesus breaks through the locked doors of our own hearts and utters that same word he uttered centuries ago, SHALOM!

Rev. Gerard J. McGlone, SJ, PhD
Georgetown University

INTRODUCTION

These reflections are the result of a silent retreat at Georgetown University, Washington, USA, in July 2019. While sitting one morning in the Dahlgren Chapel on campus, a stained glass window caught my eye and my religious imagination. Titled "The Eucharist," it was a spectacular triptych of the beloved disciple, St. John, and it led me to a meditation on Mary and her role in forming beloved disciples.

I remembered that I was installed as Archbishop of Port of Spain on December 27th, 2017, the feast of the beloved John, and that my installation on that feast became an invitation for me to also become a beloved disciple. That invitation was renewed during this retreat.

MARY'S ROLE

In the Gospels, we see Mary in the early life of Jesus and then at the crucifixion. There is little else about her. In the Synoptic Gospels (Matthew, Mark and Luke), we meet Mary only once before the Passion, when she and the family came to see Jesus (Mt 12:46-50, Lk 8:19-21, Mk 3:31-35). He did not go out to see her or invite her in. In Mark 3:21, the family came to take custody of him because they believed he was out of his mind.

Recently, I had friends and family try to take custody of me. They thought I was out of my mind because of my grueling schedule and relentless list of engagements.

There is another time when Jesus is identified as the son of Mary (Mt 13:55), but she is not part of the story.

John's Gospel is different. Mary nudges Jesus into ministry at the wedding feast in Cana. There are some interesting details here. After He resists and she insists, an incredible miracle happens. The text ends with a note that Jesus went with Mary and his family and disciples to Capernaum for a few days. After this, we do not hear about Mary until the Way of the Cross.

PRELUDE

A question emerged as I meditated on Mary and John at the cross. What was the scene like the next time Mary met those disciples who had not come to the cross? A Jewish mother, like a Caribbean mother, is not to be trifled with. It could not have been a pleasant meeting. Tradition has it that at the foot of the cross, she received the body of Jesus – the pieta. Mary was covered in blood. What did the disciples do on that Friday night and Saturday? Did Jesus appear to Mary after the resurrection? How did the disciples come to celebrate the first Eucharist? These are intriguing questions on which the *Bible* does not shed light.

For me, the most perplexing question is the one about the role of Mary. We know that she was there at Pentecost (Acts 1:14). In fact, many of our images of Pentecost have Mary at the centre of the Church. How did Mary move from obscurity in the Gospels to a central figure in the Church at Pentecost?

There are no easy answers to these questions, and these meditations do not answer them. They are simply an act of Catholic prayer and imagination (see Appendix 2). Spanning the period from Holy Thursday to Pentecost – the most formative time in the Early Church – the meditations invite readers to enter the story as if for the first time. In particular, readers are invited to dwell for a while in the Upper Room.

I asked Mary to lead me, and she led me to her way of the cross. We began on Holy Thursday with Mary knowing Jesus would be in Jerusalem. She tried to find him. She sent messages to Mary and Martha and Lazarus, but they did not know where he was either. Mary had a feeling, a mother's intuition, that all was not right. However, the other women seem to comfort her saying, "Look how they welcomed him on Sunday. All will be well."

Mary's heart was heavy during the Passover. Each prayer, each action, seemed so pointed and so real, as if this were the first Passover. This is her story of what happened next.

The text is written in the first person with Mary as our guide. I am not claiming to have had an 'apparition', nor am I claiming the status of locution or revelation. All that is being presented here is the fruit of meditation. By taking poetic licence with a text or series of events, the hope is that it will fire the Catholic imagination and move it to deeper discipleship.

The text does not answer questions of historical fact. Rather, it offers a re-reading from a fresh perspective, one that invites the modern reader/disciple to meditate again on the saving Mystery of Christ and thereby engage with Christ who is constantly knocking at their heart. I trust that when they hear him knocking, they will open the door, for he promises: "If anyone hears my voice and opens the door, I will come in and eat with him, and he with me." (Rev 3:20)

In Israel in the time of Jesus, dining was a very intimate event. You sat on the ground around a low table. You leaned back on the person next to you, steadying yourself with one hand and eating with the other hand. This intimacy is what is being promised to those who hear the knock and open the door. This intimacy is what, I pray, these meditations will ignite.

A GUIDING NOTE

Please just don't read the text (*Lectio*); enter into the scene through meditation (*Meditatio*). Spend time with the scene and start a conversation with God (*Oratio*). After this prayer, linger awhile in the Upper Room and encounter the Word who became flesh and made his home amongst us (*Contemplatio*). Readers who would like to know more about this method of prayer before entering into the text, go to Appendix 1 on *Lectio Divina*.

For readers who would like to understand more about the Catholic imagination, see Appendix 2.

For those, however, who are ready to go straight to the Upper Room to encounter Christ and the early Church, move to the next chapter.

MARY'S WAY

Late that night, John came to find me. "They took the Master," he said. I knew it! My heart had been heavy because a mother always knows when all is not well with her child. I could make no reply, so I just followed John to Caiaphas' house. As we entered, the first thing I saw was a servant girl point to Peter and say he was one of Jesus' disciples. I heard it with my own ears when Peter said: "I do not know the man." Jesus looked at him then...and loved him. I heard the cock crow and I wept, for I realised how alone Jesus must feel.

I waited there, staying in the background, until eventually they dragged Jesus out in front of everyone. He had been tortured. His eyes were swollen, and his face disfigured. A mock trial ensued, and I could see they had made up their minds to kill him. Some spoke up for him, but the chief priest and many others just shut them down. They wanted blood on this Passover night, as nothing seemed to satisfy this mob.

Early the next morning, I heard the chief priest say: "Pilate!" He made a gesture, and they dragged Jesus away, with the crowd jeering and hurling insults. All I wanted to do was to hold him and say: "It will all be ok." I tried to break free and run to him but John bid me stay. So I followed and wept silently with each step.

There, in front of Governor Pilate, I heard them shout, "Crucify him, crucify him!" My heart shattered into 10,000 pieces at these words. I could barely hold it together. I wanted so much to hug him and let him know that I loved him. I believed! I believed that God was here in this terrible mess. I believed that God would vindicate him. I believed that God, his Father, would act on his behalf. What terrible agony I felt!

Pilate tried to give Jesus a break, but the crowd was relentless. He gave in and washed his hands and then had him flogged. Each lash pierced my flesh, each stroke wounded me. Over and over. I felt his pain. He was alone, no-one to speak for him. No one to love him. I wanted to cry out, to scream out, "Don't you know who this is? This is Jesus! Stop the violence." But it remained bottled up inside. It was that kind of night, a night of terror and silence.

THE INNER CONFLICT

I remembered then the angel and what he said – that I was to conceive and bear a son, and I should call him Jesus. He was to be great, to be the son of the Most High, and the Lord would give him the throne of his ancestor David, that he would reign over the house of Jacob forever and his kingdom will have no end. I remember Simeon and Anna and their joy and sacred words. I didn't know what was true – what they had said or what was unfolding now. Them or this? It had to be one or the other; it couldn't be both. If what the angel, Simeon and Anna had said was true, God had to intervene now. I was distraught.

But I kept remembering the angel's words! With each lash Jesus received, I remembered. With each insult, I

22

remembered. I could barely breathe and I wanted to tell them: "Take me instead. Let me suffer! But please stop this madness!" His flesh was torn in every possible place. The whip sprayed his blood everywhere, including all over us. Madness took over Jerusalem that fated night and no-one could stop it. No-one tried.

They mocked him and put a crown of thorns on his head, and dressed him in a purple robe. I wept and followed as they dragged him to the cross, which they placed on his shoulder. He did not have strength, but he carried it, falling and getting back up. I felt hurt at the sight of such contempt for Jesus, who had never hurt anyone. Why did they hate him so? Why the anger? Why the violence? He was treated worse than the criminals who accompanied him. I could take it no more.

THE MEETING

The moment I saw an opening in the crowd, I ran for it. I reached right up to him, put my arms around him and told him: "Jesus, I love you. Oh, how much I want you to know that I love you. Remember the angel, remember the mysteries we shared. I love you. I believe." At that moment, time stood still. I saw in his eyes that he too believed. He also loved. His body was broken, but he believed. His eyes shone with a brightness that I would never forget.

In his gaze, I was transported to Jerusalem, to when Joseph and I presented him in the temple. I remember Simeon saying my child was to be a sign that would be rejected. I always wondered about those words because I just could not think of who might ever reject Jesus! Now on this terrible day, I was witness to the fulfilment of those words. I saw Jesus despised and rejected, and I could not comprehend how this could happen if he were God's son! Then a soldier shoved us, and the cruel spectacle was again before my eyes.

We reached the place where they would crucify him. The nails punctured his flesh with each blow of the hammer, and he winced with each stab of a nail, with each insult of the guards. Tears blurred my vision but I watched it all, each swing of the hammer, each nail being driven into his body. I had to hear each insult. I had to record in my heart what they did to my son, how they rejected him, how they mocked him. Someone had to serve as witness. Someone had to be able to recount what was done to my beautiful boy.

For what seemed an eternity. John, some other women and I stood there at the 'Place of the Skull' and looked upon Jesus in disbelief. I remembered the words of the prophet Isaiah: "He was despised and rejected." This is what they did to my son! Only a few of us witnessed this terrible scene – all the others ran away and hid.

THE EXCHANGE

Then he spoke, seven times, and each word was torture for him. I could not believe my ears when he called out to me! At the foot of the cross, he addressed me as "Woman!" Then he said, "Behold your son!" He turned to John and said, "Behold your mother." We clung to each other like never before. He held me, and I held him. It was a moment of light in the darkness of that day, relief in a torment that seemed surreal. In all his anguish and pain, Jesus still had words of love and compassion.

However, welling up in me were these terrible words: "I do not want another son. I want you, my only one." What an exchange! God's son for a disciple? I loved John, but I wanted my boy. I pleaded with God to do something! To act! To break the silence! I shouted at God: "This is our son. Where are you?" But there was no answer.

FORGIVENESS

So we remained standing there and witnessed what no-one else dared to watch. Then I heard him shout: "Father, forgive them for they know not what they do." This is my son, my beloved, my Jesus, forgiving those who tortured and condemned him to death. He had been that way from young, always the peacemaker. He eternally forgave others. But in all of this, how could he possibly forgive?

Until that moment, I had hoped that his Father would do something, that He would save him, would put those wicked people to an end and vindicate him. I waited, I watched, but Heaven was silent. I prayed, but there was no answer. Then Jesus cried out, "Eloi, Eloi, lama sabachthani!" With that, he just gave up. He was no more.

THE SILENCE

My heart exploded. No! It could not be! This could not be the end! It must be a mistake! I know what I heard from the angel! I know what the Magi said! What I saw with my eyes! I know how special he was and how precious! This could not be the end! Then the earth shook, and the ground gave way. I looked to Heaven expecting a sign, hoping God would answer. Then there was silence. There was a dead body! There was betrayal! There was a murder! Was this God's answer? Was that all He could say? Father, our son was brutally murdered, is this the best you can do?

They took Jesus down and placed him in my waiting arms. I wept with every breath I took. I cried out like a woman in travail, like Rachael weeping because her children were no more. I wept and could not be consoled. At the top of my voice, I cried to the heavens as I clung to him: "My son, my son, what have they done to you! You are God's son too!" Abba, will you really remain silent? I wept till I could cry no more. Then they took him and put him in a tomb.

THE UPPER ROOM

We had to hurry back because it was Preparation Day. We could not even do for him what the law requires or use spices to prepare him properly. We hurried because it was late and we went straight to the Upper Room where some of the others were already assembled.

My heart was empty and I felt so alone. Only I knew what the angel had said about Jesus, only I had seen those early mysteries, so it was my word against everyone else's. Only I had to hold this burden of memory, this treasure, this mystery. I held it in my broken heart and the pieces just wouldn't fit together. If Anna was right, how could this happen? If Jesus was to bring redemption to Jerusalem, how could he be dead?

THE ENCOUNTER

I had held so much in my heart all these years. Was I deluded? Did I imagine it all? Did I really see these things? For now, those questions had to wait because there was more important business to attend to.

Look at these men he chose! I told him over and over again they were no good for him. Many times I tried to rescue him because they never took care of him and now they had failed him. He taught them three long years, yet these men abandoned him in his hour of most need. I wanted to scream at them, these eleven: "Do you not know who he is? How could you abandon him in his time of great need?"

BECOMING A BLOOD MOTHER

Just then, Andrew came to me and said: "Mother, I am so sorry! I failed him!" He wept, and I cried with him. He hugged me, and I embraced him. My heart melted, and it was as if Jesus was there looking over us and loving us still. Then, one by one, they came. We embraced and wept aloud and in silent tears. His blood was all over me and, as we embraced, it was smeared all over them and their clothes and the room. From Jesus to me to them, we were all covered with his blood.

Peter came last. We approached one another in a tentative sort of way but when he was in my arms, we both wept, inconsolably. Over and over, he said: "Mother, I am sorry I let him down…I may as well have crucified him myself…He knew I would deny him, he told me so…I cannot forgive myself, I am so ashamed." I assured Peter that Jesus would forgive him. In his weakness, I found love for Peter and brought him back into the family, where he found forgiveness.

It was hard! A mother always wants to protect her son, but now I have more sons to protect. We all were blood now. In our powerlessness and pain, we were all joined in Jesus, in a mysterious but tangible way.

I thought of that scene in the Upper Room, receiving each of them, as my final act of fidelity to this silent God. He gave me the one son, who gave me the beloved disciple.

Now they all looked to me as their mother. I had no more to give.

SILENT NIGHT

We stayed in the Upper Room all of that night and all of the Sabbath. It was the first time in my life that I did not break bread on the evening of the Sabbath. The first time that I did not gather around and sing the praises of God. The first time that, on that most holy of nights, I did not cover my eyes at sunset, or say the prayer for the wine, or wash my hands, or bless the bread or the meal. Gripped by grief, we sat for the most part in silence. We had each other, and that was all. God was silent, and so was I.

FORSAKEN

As the next day unfolded, I found myself repeating Jesus' words, the ones he spoke from the cross. They were so terrible, yet so beautiful. I repeated them, at one moment drawing strength and at another being plunged into darkness. Over and over, I replayed the scene in my head. Then from nowhere, I cried out as he had: "My God, my God, why have you forsaken me?" In this prayer, this psalm, we were united, my son and I.

I began to pray aloud the psalm and others joined me, and it seemed to fill the hollowness of that day.

"My God, my God, why have you forsaken me?
Why are you so far from saving me,
so far from my cries of anguish?

My God, I cry out by day, but you do not answer,
by night, but I find no rest." (Ps 22)

The psalm gave me something to cling to. The two of us,
mother and son, could pray the same prayer – and we both
dared to pray in the face of a silent God. All of us in that
Upper Room prayed that psalm that day. We recited it from
memory and when I could not go on, the others continued
and so it went. It took all of us to pray that single psalm.

But how was I supposed to pray the ninth verse? "Yet
you brought me out of the womb; you made me trust in
you, even at my mother's breast." It was I who had taught
Jesus to walk! I who had taught him to praise God in everything. We always observed the Sabbath and every holy day.
It was I who had taught him to trust God even while he
suckled at my breast. How could this happen to my beautiful boy? How could I ever understand this terrible night? I
forced myself to recite the verse but I sobbed over every
word:

"From…birth…I…was…cast…on…you;…from…
my….mother's…womb…you…have…been…..my…
God."

Each word was like a sword in my heart, but I did not
stop. They could take my son and God could be silent, but
I would not stop praising this God.

INNER CONFLICT

As I prayed the psalm, as the others joined, the con-
flict inside me became worse. It was this God who had
sent to ask me to bear His only son. From the first

moment I knew I was pregnant, I rehearsed how I would explain the mystery of his birth. Elizabeth and I spoke about it. How do you say to a child that God is his Abba? That he is not like other children who have an Abba on earth, that God really is his Abba.

Simeon's words about Jesus being destined for the fall and rise of many haunted me. It was Jesus who had fallen, yet I could not get Simeon's words out of my head. One thing he said that was definitely true was about a sword piercing my heart. They might as well have run me through with a blade, at least that would have been merciful. I cannot bear this broken heart. In truth, I don't know what to believe, but still I will not stop my praise of "God, the King of the Universe."

LIGHT

In my utter darkness, I said the Sabbath prayer for light. I lit a candle and prayed: "Blessed are You, LORD, our God, King of the Universe, who has sanctified us with His commandments and commanded us to light Shabbat candle." I had to find a way to bring light into this darkness.

The only consolation I had was Jesus' last words, "It is accomplished." I pondered what they could mean, these words he uttered just before he died. Did he know something that I don't? He gave his all to God, did God know something? He told that thief about paradise, was there a promise made? These were my thoughts during that long Sabbath day. I was haunted, I was in grief but so too was everyone else. At least, I thought to myself, we had each other. We were bound together, the disciples and I, like never before, but it was a dark day and I struggled to find my way.

THE ANSWER

Then, early in the morning of the first day of the week, the darkness lifted. I saw him! Yes, with my own two eyes, I saw him! I was filled with such joy and light that I had no more questions for the Father. His Abba did answer after all and that was sufficient for me. My broken heart was healed that day, but it will never be the same. It was as if my eyes were opened and, for the first time, I understood the mysteries that I had lived. It was true: the Christ had to suffer and die but I could not understand that before. I had never really understood Simeon's words about a sword piercing my heart. However, at that moment of seeing him again, seeing his new body, I understood and I believed – and everything changed.

THE FIRST

After Jesus appeared to me, it was like my whole life was turned inside out – in the best way possible. We stayed in the Upper Room for long periods, each of us going and doing what was necessary only to return again, all the time eagerly expecting that new events would unfold. There was a growing sense of understanding as, slowly, we pieced together the fragments of his teaching. Little by little, we were making sense of the whole and we realised that each of us had particular fragments that we treasured.

After that glorious Sun-day when he appeared, my heart was bursting with joy, a joy I had not felt since the angel came to visit me. I knew that once again I was part of a mystery that was so big it was impossible to contain.

ENCOUNTERS

All of a sudden, there were so many sightings of Jesus that it was impossible to keep up. There was Mary Magdalene and the other women who met him early that morning, then Simon Peter and John. I went to where I was staying to change and that is where he met me. Oh, it was so beautiful that I cry each time I think about it. Then there were the two men going to Emmaus and also all the apostles, except Thomas. Each time we turned around, there was another person with a story, another episode of grace, another encounter that unlocked the mind of a disciple, and each one was so profound.

We took turns telling the story of our encounter with Jesus over and over again, telling it each time as if it was the first time. Bit by bit, we collected the stories of the various people who had seen him. I held my story in my heart and pondered it. There was so much going on, so many people speaking, so many delectable details, I was drunk with joy! It was true! I saw him, and so many others did too.

However, some of his disciples did not believe and that hurt. How could they not believe? That very evening Jesus appeared to them, but Thomas was absent. They believed then but Thomas refused to believe. I was sad that he refused to believe all of us who had seen with our eyes. Did he think we were mad or delusional? Nothing any of us said helped him believe and it was then I realised some people will never believe this mystery that we cherished so dearly. It was hard to fathom, difficult to wrap my mind around how Thomas could choose not to believe.

This is the nature of faith, I have come to learn. It is not logical, not convincing to those who refuse to be convinced, but to those who have eyes to see, it is a wonder to behold.

BELIEF AND UNBELIEF

This question of faith was central to our little community over the first few weeks, but not just because there were those who refused to believe Jesus had risen. It was also an issue among those of us who believed and knew he had risen. What did it mean that he was risen? The understanding did not come easy.

For so much of Jesus' public life, I was not involved. Mostly, I heard about what was happening from friends. Whenever I saw him, I might question him about something but I was not there for any of the healings or teachings or miracles. As we pieced together the whole, I was hearing about what my son had done, what he taught, and the impact he had on his followers.

SACRED MYSTERIES

I was in awe hearing about the beatitudes, the 'Our Father', the Kingdom of God, his times of seclusion and prayer, the many healings and his wisdom. It all boggled my mind. At home, he would always have these incredible stories with profound messages and all sorts of implications for the Law. He devoured our holy books and the teachings of the Rabbi, but this was different. It was so beautiful and holy and profound and it touched me in my deepest places. It was my turn to devour his teachings and I encouraged everyone to share as much as they could, which they did over and over in the Upper Room.

Then one day, one of them asked me, "Mother, how did all this begin?" I began to tell them about the angel and what God had said and done, about Egypt and our narrow escape there, about the many mysteries of Jesus' birth and childhood, about that day in Jerusalem when Simeon and Anna prophesied about him. They gave me their full attention as I spoke about those mysteries I had treasured in my heart.

A HARD TEACHING

On another occasion, John began to recount one of Jesus' teachings, about his body being real food and his blood real drink. I did not understand so I asked him to explain further. John said at one point, many of the disciples refused to believe this teaching because it seemed Jesus was talking about cannibalism. This sounded so unlike my son that I asked whether they were sure that was what he meant.

Peter said, "Mother, it was our most difficult day. Not only did others leave, but we also did not know what to make of this teaching. He even asked me if I was going to leave! The truth be told, I could not understand how he could say these things, how he could teach us this, but I looked into his eyes and I knew he meant every word. I did not understand his teaching, but I trusted him."

When we were alone, I asked John about it again. As much as we tried, we could not understand. It was as if we had a puzzle and major pieces were missing.

After Jesus appeared to his friends in Galilee, that time when they caught so many fish, I noticed a change in them: Peter had a new confidence, and the others began speaking more boldly and explicitly about his teachings and actions. They had new energy and purpose.

BREAD OF LIFE

The teaching on his body and blood became a focus for all of us, and we began to realise were the teachings on the Bread of Life and the last Passover were the same thing and that Jesus meant every word he had said. He really meant that the bread in the Passover became his body, and the cup of wine became his blood. Also, he had instructed the disciples to repeat this action and so make him present but no-one knew how. And, each time he appeared, they were so taken by the event that no-one asked him.

We were beginning to understand though that we would not always have him appearing to us, he intended to be present to us in a very different way. The last Passover gave his disciples power they had not understood – a means of making him present that they had not yet grasped.

Although I had hardly seen Jesus for the last three years, I longed for him now like never before. It was painful how much I wanted him with me, how much I wanted to see him, to be able to ask questions and to understand. I had a longing for him that I could not explain but it reminded me of a psalm about the doe that yearns for running streams. That is how I felt.

DO THIS IN MEMORY OF ME

One day while speaking with John about this yearning, I asked him if it were true that bread could become Jesus' body and wine could become his blood. "Please," I said, "make it happen!" The separation was driving me insane and I couldn't stand it anymore. I said to John, "Do this thing that he commanded you all to do. Do it now! I want to touch him, to hold him again. If this is the only way, do it!"

That day, some of the other women and I were gathered with John in the Upper Room. All the others had left on different errands since it was Sabbath and Jerusalem was quiet. The handful of us sat together and sang the psalms, we recalled the sacred words about Moses and the manna from Heaven. We remembered Jesus' sayings about the bread and then John took bread in his hands and prayed over it: "Blessed are You, Adonai our God, Sovereign of all, who brings forth bread from the earth…" We, our little group, responded as we did so often: "Blessed be God forever." Then John took the wine and blessed it saying: "Blessed are You, Adonai our God, Sovereign of all, creator of the fruit of the vine." Again we answered.

He began to fumble because he did not know what to do next. I could see it in his face. Then just as suddenly he became calm and looked up to Heaven as if transported there. His face became peaceful and radiant and, as he closed his eyes, I could see a transformation. A deep peace came over him and then he began: "On the night he was betrayed, Jesus took bread. And when he had given thanks, he broke it and said, 'This is my body, which is for you; do this in memory of me'. Then he took the cup, saying: 'This cup is the New Covenant in my blood; do this, whenever you drink it, in remembrance of me'."

REAL PRESENCE

It was as if all the air was sucked out of the room and the whole place was filled with Heaven. I felt as if there were angels everywhere, singing and worshipping. It was like that first night, the night of his birth when the angels filled the cave and we were transported into Heaven itself. I am sure I heard one say "Worthy is the lamb that was slain!" And another said: "Holy, Holy, Holy is the Lord God Almighty!" Light, peace and joy filled me from inside, and I bowed and worshipped. I knew God had come to visit us in that place.

I tell you, that bread was not bread. It was him. That wine was him. I should know because for nine months, I held him in my womb and then I suckled him and loved him. I tell you, that day my yearning ended. My longing ceased. This was the flesh of my flesh and the bone of my bone. I touched it with my hand and my hand knew the truth. My whole body knew the truth! This was my son, my Lord and my God, and I worshipped him!

When I received that first Eucharist, I felt full from inside. I knew this was sacred and it was not the Passover or the Shabbat meal. This was something very different. It was the way I felt when I was pregnant with Jesus. Remember, I carried him for nine long months and I was the only one who knew what it was like to have him inside. That first Eucharist felt just like that: Jesus had become flesh of my flesh, blood of my blood.

GIFT OF THE BELOVED

My son gave me the beloved disciple at the foot of the cross, and the disciple gave my son back to me. He gave me my Lord and my God! The one who took me into his home on that terrible day gave me that which was most precious. They took my son from me; John gave him back to me. He gave him as bread, he gave him as wine. On that day, I understood why Jesus gave John to me, for as he prayed those sacred words of Jesus, John was transformed. It was as if Jesus himself was there saying the words over the bread and wine. In giving me John, he gave me himself.

At the cross, in that exchange, he knew we would put the pieces of the mystery together, that my longing for him would push both of us to a deeper place of understanding. He knew we needed each other if we were to do what he asked.

NEW COVENANT

As I pondered in my heart the mystery of that first Eucharist, I remembered John had used the words, "New Covenant in my blood." It took me back to the Upper Room on that fated night and to the memory of Jesus' blood joining us. His blood, smeared over all of us, had become the healing and forgiveness we all needed. It was through his blood that each disciple was reconciled to me and each other, and it was through his blood that I became their mother. What is this New Covenant? I know the old covenants – with Adam, Noah, Abraham and David – but the prophets spoke of a New Covenant. What is this New Covenant in his blood?

Yes, he became the victim lamb, *Agnus Dei*! In the Upper Room, his blood softened my heart and invited me to become mother again. When the angel said to Joseph that the child would be Emmanuel, God with us, is this what he meant? That through the bread, God is always with us. Inside of us and acting from within? This New Covenant in his blood, what does it mean? I had so many thoughts, so many questions, yet my heart was at rest because it rested in him.

That first time was extraordinary. To touch Jesus again, to have him in me again, to be so close. I had never thought it possible. When he began his public ministry, I mourned because of my loss but I always knew he was not mine. I was worried about him, and there were times I went to get him, to rescue him. Now I realise it was he who was saving me, uniting me to Abba. A New Covenant in his blood.

Many of the women with us believed after that first Eucharist. They knew what I knew, they had touched what I touched and their eyes were opened. John also believed because I saw it in his face. He was aglow and radiant with joy. He said to me: "Mother, it was him."

I cannot explain what it was like that first time to hold Jesus again in my hands, to be joined the way we were during those nine months. It is beyond words.

I often wonder if I had not had that dark night, when they took him from me, that night of ugly violence, that night when I was stretched to the limits of faith, whether I could have seen him present in the bread and wine.

From the hands of my son, the beloved, I received my son, the Beloved. What else does he have in store for us? What else do we not yet see?

A NEW BIRTH

We spent a long time discussing these events because we were the first witnesses of this New Covenant. Though we did not understand it at the time, our hearts knew that we had stumbled upon a new dimension of our living, a depth that was not possible before. We were transfixed and filled and experienced the unity of all things. The bread and wine were him and he now fills everything. The whole world is holy!

It was only after that first Eucharist that I began to understand how close God had always been. I had heard it from the angel, but now I know it because He became bread and wine for our sake.

A NEW HEAVEN

John spoke about his experience. He said it was as if he was taken up into the seventh heaven, to a place where there was harmony, where peace flowed from all living things. There he saw one of great age sitting on a throne, with angels worshipping and bowing before him. The whole court was in worship, and every living creature was caught up in the worship of the one of great age and of the Lamb that was slain. It was, he said, the city of the living God.

When he spoke about it, I could see that he knew what I knew, that he had touched what I had touched so many years ago. John spoke about the beauty of the place and all the creatures that inhabited it. He spoke about that which no eye has seen nor ear heard, that which the human mind cannot conceive – God who was, who is and will always be. As he shared, I knew there was so much more to this incredible mystery, so much more Jesus had not told us as yet. We were barely touching the edge of the great mystery.

DESTINY

Love and peace were flowing out of John in a way I had seen so often with Jesus, like the time I told the wedding servants, "Just do what he tells you." That day joy consumed Jesus and it was infectious. I have no doubt the wine contributed but it was much more than the wine: it was about who Jesus became in that act, in the casual gesture of telling the steward to fill the jars. The steward was shocked at the new wine but I was not. I knew he would do something and oh, what a something it was!

For me, the miracle was not the water turning into wine: it was Jesus bumping into destiny! That day he crossed a threshold and he never came back. It was the day he discovered what it was all about, the day the penny dropped and insight and understanding came. I saw the same look on John's face today and knew he too had crossed a threshold. He too had discovered the plan of God hidden from all the ages, and that plan that was being revealed before our very eyes.

NEW SON

If there was a New Covenant, I said to John, then there must be a new priesthood – and he has made you a priest. This is the sacrifice of the New Covenant: he is the victim, he is the priest acting through you, and he is the spotless lamb that was slain. I could see that John was becoming another Jesus. I saw it in the Eucharist. My son John was becoming my son Jesus, who wanted me to do for John, and for all the others, what I had done for him. John was entrusted to me not so that he could take care of me but that I could take care of him, that I could lead him to the very depths of our faith, to God himself.

So began a new birth, much like the first one, and God needed me for this birth like he needed me for the first one. I began to see the hand of God in these events and realised it was the hand of my son, who is my God. That moment when he came as bread through the hands of John, a new thing happened and I rejoiced. I said, "Abba, thank you for using me again! Thank you for my son John whom you are using and who is becoming more and more like our son Jesus!"

THE BREAKING OF THE BREAD

The others returned very late that night. Although it was Sabbath and Jerusalem was quiet, some men recognised them as "that man's disciples." I could see from their faces that they were once again terrified. Many others were now gathered in the Upper Room with the 11 and Jesus' closest companions. They came in one by one and sometimes it could be as many as 120 of us gathered in the small room. Emotions would run high as we recalled every word, every gesture, every story, every event related to Jesus. We would mull it over and savour its sweetness but today there was no joy, only bitter fear in the room – and it filled the whole place.

Peter looked at me and then he looked at John. He was quick to ask: "What happened? Something happened, I can see it in your faces. Mother, tell me, did you see him again?" My heart was filled with love for Peter, for all of them. I said to him, "Yes, we met him in the breaking of the bread."

"You mean like Cleophas in Emmaus?" he asked.

I said, "No, this is different."

Jesus did not appear to us as often as before. It was well over 30 days since the first appearance and no-one had seen him for a few days. We were all terrified that he would leave us because we needed his direction. However, there would now be a new chapter in this unfolding story.

EYES TO SEE

Beginning from the start, with my intense longing for Jesus, I told them what had happened, how it was always Jesus' intention to remain with us, not in his physical body like we have seen him so often in this last month, but in a new form.

Then I spoke about Abraham and his encounter with Melchizedek, the priest of Salem who offered a sacrifice of bread and wine; Moses and the manna from Heaven that fed the people for four long years; the Passover which we had just celebrated where the flesh of the lamb is food for the journey and the sprinkling of the blood on the lintel of the doorpost allowed the angel of death to pass over our houses; and about our celebration of the Todah where we give God thanks for deliverance and use bread and wine as sacrifice and thanksgiving. These were the mysteries in which we were immersed in the breaking of the bread and the pouring out of the wine.

Their fear turned into complete excitement again. "Could it be true?" James cried out.

"Could it be true?" I replied. Then I recounted what I had experienced in that first Eucharist and how the room was filled with angels singing.

John spoke about his vision of the New Heaven and the New Earth. He said God intended to dwell amongst his people, that we were like a bride prepared for Jesus, that God himself intends to be our God and for us to be his people. He spoke of the moment when he knew that Jesus had given himself to us as bread and wine and made the disciples priests of the New Covenant. John said: "It is through our hands that he intends to come and dwell amongst us, dwell within us." Then he spoke about the marriage feast of the Lamb, the supper where we will be filled to overflowing, like the meal on the mountain in the Book of Isaiah where there is plenty of good food and fine wine. The difference at this meal is that the food is Jesus' body and the drink is his blood.

MEMORIA

John continued: "Peter, do you remember when we were by the Sea of Tiberias and Jesus spoke about the living bread? He said, 'Unless you eat of my body and drink of my blood you will not have life in me'. Do you remember that many left him? Do you remember he asked you if you would leave him also?"

Peter recalled the day. "It was as if he wanted us to become cannibals," he said. They all remembered that difficult teaching, how awkward it was, how he explained it more explicitly. They remembered too that some tried to reduce it to a figure of speech.

Then Andrew said: "Do you remember Jesus changed the word 'to eat' from *phago* to *trogo* when they challenged him about cannibalism? He went from 'spiritual eating' to 'tearing of the flesh'."

Nathaniel exclaimed: "That's it! In that ancient meal, we remember the passing of the angel of death over the houses of our forefathers because of the blood of the lamb. We remember it was the flesh of the lamb and the unleavened bread that fed us and gave our ancestors strength to pass from death to life. In the Passover we say, 'It is as if you were present in Egypt'. Remember at our last meal with Jesus told us, no he instructed us, he commanded us: 'Do this in memory of me'. It is true! He intends the bread to be his flesh and the wine to be his blood. He intends to be with us in this way."

We continued like this, with all of the disciples adding to the story, each one seeing a gem in a fragment of memory. Piecing the fragments together, precious piece by precious piece, we wove a tapestry of meaning that night. Collectively, we came to understand the sacred mystery in which we all participated. We saw it with new eyes, as if for the first time. Jesus had intended to be with us in the breaking of the bread. I knew this in my heart and the disciples knew it now in every part of their being.

MY LORD AND MY GOD

It was very early on the first day of the week and still dark. John led the singing of the psalms, then they all participated in reading the Holy Scriptures, recalling how it was said that the Christ must die for the forgiveness of sins. Cleophas recounted what Jesus said to him and the other disciple on the road to Emmaus, about Moses and all the prophets. Cleophas recalled how Jesus explained that all the scripture pointed to him and that they recognised him in the breaking of the bread.

There were songs of thanksgiving and prayers offered up to God. There was excitement in the air, like fire! Then Peter took the bread and gave thanks. He blessed it and broke it. He said the sacred words. He did the same with the cup. My heart was filled with a love that was so pure. It was for love that I was pierced! For love that my heart was broken! Now I saw that prophecy by Simeon differently: my heart, having been pierced by the violence against Jesus, was now pierced by his incredible presence. Through that wound, he entered my heart and filled it with himself. The Eucharist was pure ecstasy. I was wounded by love, and I worshipped him – my Lord and my God!

BIRTHING

After we stumbled into the breaking of the bread and Jesus' real presence, the Eleven began to change. The first time Peter broke the bread, they were all transfixed and afterwards they had a certain presence that I had only ever seen in Jesus. They began growing into him and it was so incredible to see. They were each becoming my son; I had become their mother. I was doing for them what I had done for my son Jesus; I was teaching them the mysteries of God, and they were being transformed.

At the moment when Peter broke the bread, they prayed in pure silence. No words, no gestures, it was as Jesus had once said, "in Spirit and truth." When each received, they believed. They knew in that secret place that it was him: he was the bread, the bread was him. They worshipped, and then Peter lifted the cup and said the sacred words and, again, Jesus filled the entire room. And, each person partaking of the cup was filled with him.

TRANSFORMATION

We spent a long time in silence after partaking of the cup. We had him. We knew it and no-one could take that from us. My son came to each of his disciples as bread and wine. Who could believe it? But he did, and it was beautiful. My most precious memory of that first time with the whole group was to see them becoming like

Jesus, to see them slowly grasping what he taught and what he expected of them. There was no fear anymore; instead, a growing boldness.

Our conversations changed. Not only were we collecting memories, we were also looking at implications. We were looking at Jesus' expectations of us and began to understand that we were connected to him in a new and very different way. It was John who said one day: "Remember, he told us on the night before he died that we were like branches of the vine. What if he really meant this not as an image or symbol, but what if this is how we are actually connected to him? In the Eucharist, he is in us. We know we received him. He promised that he would abide in us and he does. He lives in us in the bread we eat and in the cup we drink. We know it is him. We are in him as he is in us, and we are to be him to the world."

Nathaniel recalled: "Remember, he said that we will do greater things than he. At the time, I thought that was madness but what if he meant that, with he in us and us in him, we would be able to act as he did and live as he lived – and become him!"

Philip added: "When I took the bread in my hands, I just knew it was the holiest thing I had ever held. Then I realised it was him; he was the holiest thing I had ever held! I realised then he had always been special, not just a teacher, a Rabbi, but something more. Peter, do you remember when he asked us who the crowds were saying he was? And how he then wanted to know who we thought he was? Peter, you told him, 'You are the Christ, the son of the living God'. Peter, it is true! Jesus is the Christ! He is God! Only God could do what he did."

Rebirth

This was a glorious time as these men began to under-stand and to see with new eyes. They became emboldened, and now there was no stopping them. It was like a birth! One of them, I think it was James, said: "Remember what he told Nicodemus? 'Unless you are born again, you cannot be my disciple'." Is this what he meant? There was indeed a rebirth and I was there to witness Jesus being born again. On both occasions when he came into the world, I was there. Both times God asked me to do the impossible and both times I knew it was God! I knew the sacredness of the moment and I knew what he asked of me.

A few days later, the Eleven received a message to meet Jesus in Bethany and they set off to meet him. I and some of the other women remained in Jerusalem. The Upper Room was filthy because we had been there for many days. We cleaned it and while cleaning, we spoke about how rich our lives had become. Again and again, we recounted the events from that terrible night to now. We chatted about how our little family had grown in perception and love. Suzanna, who had accompanied the disciples on some of their travels, said to me: "Mother, I do not know what they would have done without you." We all laughed.

Be Mother

On that morning when I met him, when he came to me with the holes in his hands, he said one thing to me: "They need a mother." That was all. He had the biggest smile on his face, there pure joy in his eyes, and that was enough for me. I really thought it was a dream or, worse, that I was going mad, but I could not get the words out of my head, I could not get the scene out of my mind.

When I woke up that morning, I realised that Mary Magdalene and the other Mary were not there. The spices we had collected were missing, so I assumed they had gone to the tomb. I had asked them to wake me so I could go with them, but they went without me. I had been intending to leave for Nazareth that day because I felt I had done what I could and now I needed a quiet place to grieve and to ponder all that had happened. I just wanted to get out of this terrible city. I was actually packing my bags when Jesus came and told me my role as mother had not ended. So, that is why I stayed.

The events that have unfolded in these days have been for me the most beautiful in my life. Giving birth to him all those years ago was very special but now I feel as if I have given birth to so much more. Just when I thought it had all been for no use, God stepped in again and brought life where there was death. It has been like giving birth to him over and over again.

A CHURCH

The apostles returned from Bethany overjoyed. They had spoken with Jesus at length about the breaking of the bread and his presence, about the cup and the New Covenant. They talked about their new role and his expectations. He wanted them to go into the whole world and preach the Good News to all creation. These men returned with great excitement; they were reborn. They were on fire for him. They would have done anything he asked.

The fear had gone and, with it, the hesitation, the doubt and the worry. All of us were rejoicing and singing praise to God, the King of the Universe. I had been wrong about these men. At first I just could not see what Jesus saw in them, but I did not have the whole picture. As events unfolded, it was clear to me that he had picked well, that these were the men to do what he asked. He told them that they must stay in Jerusalem and wait to be clothed with power from on high. He spoke to them about the Holy Spirit.

During this time, Peter added Matthias to their number. Also, there was much talk about Jesus' command to preach the Good News to all creation. They went back and forth and the conversation would always end with them saying: "Yes, yes, we know we need to wait till it happens to fully understand."

Holy Spirit

I asked them what Jesus said about the Holy Spirit and they looked at each other blankly. They clearly did not think much about it, but afterwards began recounting the various things he had said to them about the Holy Spirit.

Andrew spoke up: "I was there when John baptised him, I was there when he came up out of the water and a dove appeared and landed on him. Afterwards, I asked my master what that was about. He told all of us that was the Holy Spirit. After that, he pointed me to Jesus, he called him Lamb of God. John insisted to us that Jesus was the Christ but he never told us anything more about the Holy Spirit."

Matthew said: "Remember what he taught after giving us the 'Our Father'? He said if we who are evil know how to give good things to our children when they ask, how much more will the Father give the Holy Spirit to those who believe!" He continued: "When he taught us to pray, he also taught us about the Holy Spirit, that we should ask the Father to send us the Holy Spirit."

They all agreed that they must wait, watch and pray.

John added: "It was as if he was preoccupied with the Holy Spirit in his last days. He spoke of the Holy Spirit as counsellor, guide. Jesus even said he would send us another advocate, the Spirit of Truth, who will lead us to the full truth, who will remind us of everything he taught us. But he also said to us that the Spirit will teach us what is to come."

James said: "Yes, but it was conditional. I remember him saying, 'If you love me, you will obey what I command and I will ask the Father, and he will send his Holy Spirit'."

James continued: "He made a claim I did not understand, that the Father, the Son and the Spirit will come to us and they will live in us." He asked the others if they remembered, and they all did.

THE CONCEPTION OF JESUS

It was John who then asked me about the Holy Spirit: "When you spoke about the birth of Jesus, you mentioned the Holy Spirit." "Oh yes, I did!" I replied. I told them how amazing it was, how the angel delivered his message and I responded: "Do unto me according to your word." No sooner had the words left my mouth, I said to them, I had an encounter about which I have never spoken, an experience that was delightful and terrifying at the same time.

I explained: "I felt this gentle, warm presence filling me. So tender was the touch that if I was not paying attention, I could have missed it, but it was overwhelmingly real. I felt like I was connected to every living creature. I could feel the joy and the pain of all who lived. I wanted to laugh, I wanted to cry. The presence felt expansive, beyond me, and yet it was present to me, asking permission to move on at every stage.

"At each movement, I consented, and as I consented, there was another movement. I was becoming known better than I knew myself. I was being loved more perfectly. I was alive and whole and filled and overflowing. Yet I had to continually say 'yes' at each step, and it seemed that my 'yes' and the presence worked in complete harmony. The more I said 'yes', the more I was filled, and the closer I felt to God. The Holy Spirit is bold in its actions but also shy.

"When I arrived at Elizabeth's home she cried out in excitement and said the child leapt in her womb. In that meeting, I felt like I would burst into speech or song at any moment. I remember saying 'yes' over and over and then I heard myself praise God in a beautiful cascade of words: 'My soul magnifies the Lord, and my spirit rejoices in God, my saviour'."

I repeated all of the words to them but, more than that, I had wanted them to hear about the tenderness and shyness of the Holy Spirit.

A GOOD MOTHER

I said to them that the Spirit is like a good mother, who leads her children by leading-strings of love. She is so gentle that the slightest rejection will cause her to stop and wait. There is no imposing anything, no fleeing but just waiting, waiting on an opening, a 'yes'! Once that 'yes' is given, she will make haste and do all that is required. As we say 'yes' to the Holy Spirit, her actions become bold.

It realised that what God did in my body through the Holy Spirit, God now intended to do to the Twelve. In fact, to all of us. I tried to remember the way the Holy Spirit had acted in me, the way we had worked together to get to this point.

James asked if the Spirit was the Father coming in a different form. Instinctively, I said no. This is not the Father! This is like a very different part of God. I could not say how, but I knew my relationship with the Holy Spirit was very different from the relationship I had with Abba.

Then Matthew said: "He commanded us to baptise in the name of the Father and Son and the Holy Spirit." What could that mean? We mused over it for a long while. What we knew from Andrew was that Jesus was to baptise with water and the Holy Spirit, which was different to John's baptism.

EMPTY YOURSELF

I told them my encounters with the Father and the Holy Spirit had taught me one thing: there is no movement towards God if pride is present. I said: "To prepare for the Holy Spirit, humility is the key. We have to learn to empty ourselves so God can fill us. In my experience, being filled by the Holy Spirit is not like pouring a liquid into a container, where the container gives the shape to the liquid. It is more than that. There is a dynamic between the liquid and the container, whereby God not only fills but God transforms what he fills. God wants to change each of us into His presence here on earth. Just think about the breaking of the bread: when you received it, was that it? Did it end there?"

They all agreed that there was more to it, that we were becoming like Him in a most dramatic way. If through the bread and the cup we were transformed, the Spirit would do similar work, I told them, because God wants to fill us with the utter fullness of Himself. Our transformation by the Spirit would be greater. I don't know how, but I do know that God always has a great plan.

Preparation

We spoke for many days about the Holy Spirit in that Upper Room and I realised they needed me to help them prepare, to help them understand and be ready for what Jesus wanted of them. I was the only one who had experience with the Holy Spirit and so I was the one forming them for the greatest adventure of their life. As we remembered Jesus' commission, we all became more emboldened to do what he asked. As we spoke, it was as if he was with us. Something powerful was happening in the upper room in those days.

One day I told them that what the Spirit did in me to bring forth Jesus, the Spirit would now do in each of them. If he is the vine and we the branches, then we are connected to him and to each other. There is something that God wants, I could feel it.

When I became the mother of Jesus, God became his father, and I became the spouse of God. I sense that He wants a relationship of complete loving, giving and relating, just like a spousal relationship. The outpouring of the Holy Spirit is more than a filling up; it is God and us becoming one, just as in the Eucharist.

Pentecost Day

I was so excited I could barely sleep at night. Then it happened. On the first day of the week, we awoke early and sang the psalms and praised the God of our fathers who raised Jesus our Lord from death to life. We recounted the Scriptures. Our hearts burned that day as the Twelve went through everything the Scriptures told about the Holy

Spirit. Then there was the breaking of the bread and the raising of the cup. He came to us, and it was so amazing. Each of us was filled to the utter fullness and aglow with pure love and light. Then there was a violent wind and fire came from Heaven and rested on our heads. I had had that experience before and recognised it as the Holy Spirit. God had sent the Holy Spirit, and there was a new boldness in each person in that Upper Room.

I understood that God had a plan of which I was a part, a tiny part. My 'yes' allowed Jesus to come to us and live among us. It also allowed us to discover the breaking of the bread, that pivotal event that renewed our hope and revived us at our lowest moment. Now, God plans to form us into a body, one single body with the Spirit animating us into life. I was overjoyed to see the transformation in the Twelve and in all of the disciples. I had been able to do for them what I had done for my son Jesus, so they are all my children now.

With the coming of the Holy Spirit, the Twelve began public ministry. As happened in Jesus' life, I went into the shadows again. I was never worried about them the way I was worried about Jesus. It was not because I loved them less; I loved each of them like I loved Jesus. I would die for any one of them. I was not worried because I understood so much more now. I knew that they were in God's hands, for they were His children too. They would be looked after by Father, Son and Holy Spirit.

CONCLUSION

I hope these meditations in the Upper Room have opened for you a new portal through which to encounter Christ. Every Christmas we celebrate Mary, whom we know to be the mother of Jesus. In Luke's Gospel (Lk 2:1-20), we read the account of the annunciation, visitation and Jesus' birth. We also know that Mary is the mother of the beloved disciple (Jn 19:25-27). In this, Jesus intended Mary to have a mother's role in the life of the beloved.

We also believe that Mary is the mother of the apostles and mother of the Church. She had the most intimate relationship with Father, Son and Holy Spirit. That intimacy and experience would have been a great blessing to the apostles as they fumbled through the sacred mysteries.

The transformation of the disciples in the New Testament is remarkable. They move from a scattered band of cowards to courageous proclaimers of Christ. This happens between Holy Thursday and Pentecost, so understanding this time is crucial to understanding the transformation that the Church of today needs to experience.

Once more, our doors are locked for fear of the Jews. Once more, we are huddling and terrified. Once more, there is a hostile world out there that wants to destroy us. Once more, the apostles—bishops, priest and leaders—have messed up badly and disappointed Jesus. We have, once more, found ourselves on the wrong side of the crucifixion.

The close connection between our current context and that of the Upper Room on Good Friday must not be overlooked. It is this connection between the Church of today and the Early Church that gave birth to these meditations.

The disciples found their way from despair to hope, from cowardice to courage, from saving their life to giving it away. So must we! It is clear, however, that the transformation was not the initiative of the apostles. God initiated the unfolding mystery and that is why they had to sit and wait and pray.

We too must sit and wait and pray in the Upper Room. We also must allow Mary to become our mother. What she did for the first disciples, she wants to do for us. Meet her in the upper room, let her lead you to the rebirth that God intends for His children of this time.

POSTSCRIPT

Then Mary said to me: "To become a beloved disciple, meet me in the Upper Room. Meet me when all hope is dashed, and all joy is gone. Meet me when God is silent, when you know your frailty, when you cannot see, when you cannot believe. Then, in that Upper Room, I will teach you how to become a beloved disciple. Through His blood, I will teach you how to become my son, how to become a son of God."

A prayer reflection in Dahlgren Chapel, Georgetown University, Washington, USA, July 12-14, 2019

APPENDIX 1

Lectio Divina

Lectio Divina is a process of unfolding. First comes the *Lectio*, the reading of the sacred text. This is done several times slowly, prayerfully and in a meditative way. We are meant to savour the sweetness of the words, and to hear not just the words but the Word who became flesh and dwelt amongst us. This is prayer: opening the heart to Jesus who is knocking, and looking for the Word who is there in the midst of the words we are reading. Scripture is like a sacred portal; by reading with faith and expectation, the sacred door opens, and we are allowed into the next chamber.

In the *Meditatio*, we are invited to mull over what we've read or heard. Begin by noticing some element of the text that strikes you, either a word, phrase or a person. It is here that the sacred door opens, so follow the Holy Spirit who guides. Allow yourself to be led deeper and deeper into the depths of the text. Move around in your mind the word, phrase or person that struck you and go deeper. Ask new questions: How does the passage speak to the text of my life? What in the text is asking a question of me, or challenging me? What am I drawn to in this text, and why?

Through a series of interrogations led by the Spirit and the curiosity of our religious imagination, we begin to enter into the passage more deeply and end up inhabiting the text for a while. We bring all of ourselves to the scripture and allow all of the Word to encounter all of us.

The third step in the process is *Oratio*. Silently, respond to God in prayer, with the text as the background or foreground for the conversation. The conversation can take many forms. As you and God engage each other it allows for wrestling, for God invites us to ask our most profound questions. We move from text to encounter, from the words to the Word who becomes flesh and dwells amongst us. It is Christ himself that we seek in this part of the process. By listening to Christ and engaging him in silence and prayer, we are moved to the next stage.

The fourth step is *Contemplatio*. This is when the soul is led beyond words to rest in God. The soul experiences the sweetness of being 'in Christ'. Rest awhile here, allow God to renew and love you in this moment. As the author of the Book of Hebrews says: "But you have come to Mount Zion, to the city of the living God, the heavenly Jerusalem."

IGNATIAN PRAYER

The Ignatian method of praying with the scriptures is very similar to *Lectio Divina*. The one significant difference is in the *Meditatio*, St Ignatius asks that we close our eyes and picture ourselves in the biblical scene. Enter into it like a movie. Look, smell and taste, feel the energy and observe the interaction of the characters. In doing so it becomes a living text and you are invited to experience it from the inside. This leads you to have conversations with the characters.

Having attended Ignatian retreats for many years, this method of prayer appeals to me. It has been the mainstay of my spiritual odyssey. The end result of this method is encountering Christ in the *Contemplatio*. It also helps you to meditate more deeply on the scriptures and delve below the surface. It was by meditating on the stained-glass window of Mary receiving the Eucharist that these meditations in the Upper Room were born. I invite you to engage the scriptures or a sacred image and move slowly through the steps of the Ignatian prayer process.

Jesus is waiting to encounter you.

APPENDIX 2

RELIGIOUS IMAGINATION

Sitting before this spectacular triptych is where this book began. The stained-glass window is a fine example of religious imagination at play. It depicts something unusual, and also answers legitimate questions...that had been waiting to be asked!

The first panel is a scene from the Last Supper, with the beloved disciple leaning against Jesus in the intimate posture that we know well. The middle panel shows Mary and the beloved disciple at the foot of the Cross. This is also very traditional. The third panel depicts the beloved disciple giving Communion to Mary. This captured my attention and imagination. Of course! Mary must have received the Eucharist! Is it in the *Bible*? No. Would it have happened? But of course! Mary was part of the Early Church. We believe she lived with St John in Ephesus, partly because of a house and chapel there. Would Mary have gone to Mass? Absolutely!

So naturally, the window invited me to a meditation on Mary and her role in forming beloved disciples.

Over the three panels is a round window with the Eucharist in the centre, a reminder of the title and focus of the triptych. Since ancient times, the Eucharist has been considered as a memoria of two moments in the life of Christ – the Last Supper and Good Friday. The first moment is the betrothal of the Bride, the Church, to the Bridegroom, Christ. The second moment is the consummation of the marriage of the Lamb to his Bride, the Church. The understanding of Christ as bridegroom is very ancient, and Jesus also gave himself that designation. In Matthew, Mark, Luke and John, Jesus speaks about the bridegroom, referring to himself and his ministry (fasting and the bridegroom, Mt 9:14-16; Mk 2:18-20; Lk 3:33-35; the foolish and wise virgins, Mt: 25:1-13; and the wedding feast of Cana, Jn 2:8-10.)

For more on this, see Brant Pitre's book, *Jesus the Bridegroom*.

Thank you for accompanying me in the Upper Room. I pray that you have been strengthened by your sojourn there. Enter Mary's heart, she will lead you to Jesus.

Made in the USA
Columbia, SC
19 November 2020